Bradwell's Book of Cornwall

a Feast of **Fun, Facts** and **History!**

Published by Bradwell Books
11 Orgreave Close Sheffield S13 9NP
Email: books@bradwellbooks.co.uk

Compiled by Camilla Zajac

All rights reserved. No part of this publication may be reproduced, stored in a retrieval system or transmitted in any form or by any means, electronic, mechanical, photocopying, recording or otherwise without the prior permission of Bradwell Books.

British Library Cataloguing in Publication Data:
a catalogue record for this book is available from the British Library.

1st Edition

ISBN: 9781912060580

Design & Typesetting by: Andrew Caffrey

Print: Gomer Press, Llandysul, Ceredigion SA44 4JL

Photograph Credits: iStock, Creative Commons and credited individually.

Cover Images Credits: Main iStock
Left to right. Andrew & Susan Caffrey, iStock, iStock, Helston Museum, iStock, iStock

Bradwell's Book of Cornwall

a Feast of Fun, Facts and History!

BRADWELL BOOKS

Contents

INTRODUCTION
Introducing Cornwall, the most remote county in the UK, but with an influence which reaches around the world and as well-loved for its famous pasties as it is for its stunning scenery and strong sense of identity.

CORNISH WIT AND HUMOUR
The Cornish are known for their sense of humour. In this section you will find humorous tales and jolly jokes connected with the area and its people.

CORNISH LEGENDS
Cornwall is associated with legends of many kinds. It's not hard to see why. From its connection with the most famous legendary king to tales of the little people and the county's mysterious standing stones, this is a place where legend endures.

CORNISH HISTORY
Cornwall has a rich and fascinating history. From its time as a leader in the industrial world to the story of the Cornish diaspora, the county has shaped the world in many ways.

CORNISH GHOSTS
Cornwall's landscape is packed full of creepy tales of ghostly apparitions and spirits from times long past. Not surprisingly, the Cornish coast has given rise to many otherworldly tales.

CORNISH RECIPES
The recipes of Cornwall are a part of its culinary heritage. The food experienced in the Duchy is one of the most talked-about subjects for locals and for those visiting on holiday. Cornwall's cuisine reflects the rich tapestry of its history.

THE CORNISH LANGUAGE

The Cornish language has a fascinating history. Cornish is one of six Celtic languages, brought over when the Celts migrated across to Britain and Ireland from mainland Europe. Try speaking some Cornish words and phrases for yourself!

FAMOUS LOCALS

Cornish locals have had an influence on areas as diverse as music, mathematics, sport and science. With so many local people helping to shape life in the UK and further afield, we share just some of Cornwall's movers and shakers from past and present.

CORNISH CUSTOMS

As a county rich in history, Cornwall has some fascinating customs, a number of which are kept alive to this day. From the Helston Floral Day to its sham mayors, it is a place where dancing, singing and general merriment continue to form an important aspect of its identity.

FAMOUS CORNISH MURDERS

Two of Cornwall's historic murders are still talked about to this day. One because it involves a famous author and has an unnerving psychic twist; the other because it was a tragic tale which inspired a well-known author to pen a ballad.

LOCAL NAMES

Cornwall is not only the base for a number of nationally and internationally well-loved brands, it is also the source of inspiration for companies in sectors as varied as fashion, food and water sports.

CORNISH SPORTS

With such strong roots in its past, it is perhaps not surprising that Cornwall has some fascinating sporting traditions with enduring associations with its history. Whether it is wrestling or windsurfing, the sports which are big in Cornwall are closely connected with its heritage and landscape.

Introduction

What Do You Associate with Cornwall? Is it the Famous Cornish Pasty? The Stunning Scenery? The Intriguing History?

There is no doubt that Cornwall is a place of many aspects, and that the more you get to know it, the more there is to know.

Many people think of holidays, sunshine and ice cream when they think of Cornwall. That's not surprising with tourism contributing up to 24 per cent of Cornwall's gross domestic product. Cornwall has the longest coastline of any English county, measuring over 400 miles or nearly 700 kilometres! It's one of the most remote parts of the UK but, at 1,376 square miles, it makes up a pretty large chunk of the country.

There's no doubt that Cornwall has faced challenges, for example the high levels of unemployment and being one of the poorest areas in the UK while having some of the country's highest living costs. Yet, despite these problems, Cornwall continues to be known and loved as a place for fun activities such as surfing and walking.

It is also associated with artistic endeavours and fictional worlds. Cornwall is a place of contrasts. While it is now seen as a place of escape by many, it was once a centre of industry. Although it is valued as an area where a more natural way of life can be enjoyed, it is also now giving rise to businesses which are shaping industries across the globe. That's why we can only scratch the surface of Cornwall in this book. It is a place that has fascinated people for many, many years and will continue to do so long into the future. Remote and isolated from much of the country, Cornwall continues to fight for its own identity to this day. No wonder its motto is

'One and All'

In this book, we take a brief journey through Cornwall's rich history and how locals have successfully fought to make the Cornish an independent ethnic group. We also find out about the Cornish Alps and the interesting history behind them. One of the things Cornwall is particularly known for is its heritage of weird stories and fascinating superstitions. Once upon a time, Cornwall was the land of giants and the little people, the piskies. Read on to take a wander around its landscape and discover the stirring stories behind its standing stones. We will also explore the ghosts which are said to inhabit the land, from phantom coaches to headless horsemen. We look at Cornwall's connection with probably the most famous legendary king and the fascinating link between Cornish people and a certain bird.

Cornwall is a county with its own unofficial national anthem. It's a place where people proudly fight for their rights and their identity. While Cornwall is certainly changing and has many exciting times ahead, it also has strong connections with its past. While the tales of its old customs may sound like they are part of history, some of those traditions are still lovingly kept alive by locals to this day. It is the same too for the county's language: *'Kernowek'* has come a long way since it was brought over when the Celts migrated across to Britain and Ireland from mainland Europe, continuing to be spoken in Cornwall, the Isles of Scilly and in West Devon and Exeter until its fall at the Reformation. After nearly becoming lost in the mists of time, the Cornish language is now enjoying a resurgence.

There's no doubt about it – Cornwall is a place it takes time to really get to know. Yes, it is famous for its pasties, its beaches and its holiday fun. But there is much, much more to it than that. This little book can only go so far in telling those stories. But hopefully we have shared some of the mystery, the history and the ways of life which go into making Cornwall one of the most fascinating places in the world.

Read on to see for yourself!

'Cornwall is very primeval: great, black, jutting cliffs and rocks, like the original darkness, and a pale sea breaking in, like dawn. It is like the beginning of the world, wonderful...'

D.H. LAWRENCE

Cornish History

What's in a Name?

From where does Cornwall get its distinctive name? It is thought that the name is derived from a tribal name, the Cornovii, also known as **'The Horn People'**, the horn being a reference to the shape of the region in which they are located, making them **'Peninsula People'**. It is believed that part of the word *wealas* was added by the Anglo-Saxons. This means *'foreigner'* or *'Roman'*.

In the Cornish language, Cornwall is called 'KERNOW', which is believed to be derived from a similar background to the name of the Cornovii.

A Fascinating Past

The first people to live in Cornwall were hunter–gatherers in about 10,000 BC. We can thank the people of the Bronze Age for the many fascinating standing stones and megalithic sites seen in the landscape of Cornwall to this day. As well as creating many interesting landmarks, the people of the Bronze Age settled in the area and started farming it. It was during the first millennium AD that the place we know today as Cornwall developed from the Roman division of territory. This is when it started to become known by its Late British name, **Cornouia**, which means the land of the Cornovii. Then Cornouia became *Cornubia* (Latin), *Cernyw* (Welsh) and *Kernow* (Cornish). The area began to develop a language of its own.

The Crow of Cornwall

What do King Arthur, a member of the crow family and the pride of a region have in common?

Quite a lot, actually. It's all about the Cornish chough. This fascinating bird is the symbol of Cornwall. You can find it on the Cornish coat of arms, but you will also notice it in all manner of settings promoting proud local businesses.

So why the chough? Well, it is closely associated with the Duchy of Cornwall and has been for hundreds of years. 'Chough' was also once used as a nickname for Cornish people. Back in the 17th century, in Wales and Scotland, the bird was referred to as 'the crow of Cornwall'. The legend goes that when King Arthur died, he turned into a chough, with the bird's red beak and feet symbolising his violent death. Sadly, this legendary association did not protect the chough from declining significantly in numbers after the Second World War due to changes in farming practices which affected insect numbers. By the early 1900s, the chough was no longer to be seen in the UK, apart from in Cornwall, with sightings dwindling completely after the 1970s. These days, the story of Cornwall's emblem is a much happier one, thanks to the natural return of choughs to Cornwall in 2001, when a group of three birds were seen living on the Lizard peninsula.

In 2002, two of the birds raised young, the first in Cornwall in more than fifty years! Since 2002, 88 chicks have fledged from Cornish nests.

Perran Beach in Perranporth - iStock

St. Piran

St. Piran's Day is the national day of the people of Cornwall. It is held on 5 March every year. Named after one of the patron saints of Cornwall, the day started as one of the tin miners' holidays in the late 19th and early 20th centuries. It is said that a great deal of food and alcohol was enjoyed during what was known back in tin-mining days as *'Perrantide'*. No wonder the phrase *'drunk as a perraner'* was used in 19th-century Cornwall to refer to people who had consumed copious quantities of alcohol! The day after St. Piran's Day also had a name: **Mazey Day**. Celebrating St. Piran's Day had a resurgence in the 1950s. Nowadays, many Cornish communities mark the occasion.

Born in Ireland, the man who was to become St. Piran was made a bishop after studying the scriptures in Rome. He started to perform miracles, which amazed many people. However, this was not well received by the kings of

Cornish Flag
iStock - Lance B

Ireland and he was thrown into the sea with a millstone around his neck. Incredibly, he floated to Perran Beach in Perranporth, where he duly built a chapel. One day, he set up a fire. A black stone on the fire started to leak white liquid when it became hot. This little accident was the discovery of tin, a metal which would shape the history of Cornwall for centuries to come. St Piran became the patron saint of Cornwall and of tin miners. He is celebrated on the Cornish flag, which is also known as the flag of St. Piran. The flag's design of a white cross on a black background symbolises white tin from black rock and good triumphing over evil.

Cornwall has two other patron saints – St. Michael (associated with St. Michael's Mount and celebrated on 8th May) and St. Petroc (associated with Padstow and celebrated on 4th June).

ains at Levant Tin Mine - iStock

Cornish INDUSTRY

Walk along the Cornish coast and you will discover many clues to its fascinating industrial past. The picturesque ruins of tin-mining buildings which mark the landscape are clues to the rich history of tin mining in Cornwall. Some people say that if you look at any hole in the ground in the world, you will discover a Cornishman searching for metal! That's no wonder when you consider that mining has been a tradition in Cornwall for more than a thousand years. Well before records began, Cornish people were working hard at picking copper and tin from the ground. This turned into a world-recognised expertise in mining. By the time of the gold rush in the USA, miners from Cornwall were thought to be some of the world's best hard-rock miners.

Botallack Tin Mine - iStock - Chrisdorney

It was with the coming of steam power that the combination of Cornwall's richness of resources and its people's skills at exploiting them really gained traction.

The huge steam engines which were first created by **Boulton and Watt** enabled underground shafts to be dug much deeper and to be kept dry using pumps. By the start of the 19th century, Cornish mines were right at the cutting edge of the Industrial Revolution. The British copper industry was focused on West Cornwall, with tin mining also hugely successful in the area. This industry created communities and established ways of life and customs, some of which still survive today. Cornwall became one of the most abundant mining areas in that period, with Gwennap referred to as *'the richest square mile on earth'*, having reserves of tin and copper valued at around ten million pounds!

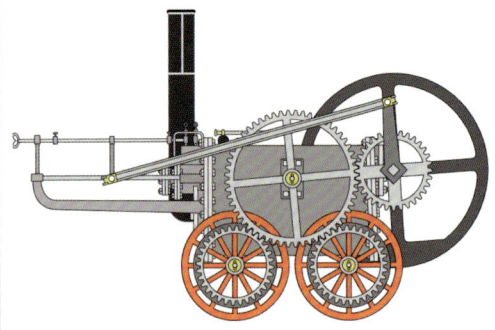

Trevithick Steam Locomotive – CC Urizzato

Cornwall's mining success was nurtured by innovations from locals, such as Cambourne man RICHARD TREVITHICK (who designed the first high-pressure steam engine and the first full-scale working railway steam locomotive), Penzance local SIR HUMPHRY DAVY (the miners' safety lamp) and Redruth's WILLIAM MURDOCH (the first to experiment with gas for domestic lighting).

The 19th century also saw Cornwall associated with another important contribution to industry – china clay.

China Clay Pit St. Austell - iStock

China clay was originally used in ancient China to make beautifully fine white porcelain and after pieces were brought to Europe, porcelain became highly prized. In the 1700s, a Plymouth apothecary called WILLIAM COOKWORTHY spent several years searching for a material that resembled the kaolin used in the Chinese ceramics and succeeded in finding the answer – a rare type of decomposed granite at Tregonning Hill, near Germoe, known locally as Moorstone, Growan or Growan Clay. Cookworthy found a way to separate and process it to make porcelain, after which he set up the Plymouth Porcelain Factory and started manufacturing fine china. By the early 19th century, the industry was very well established with St. Austell in Cornwall as the centre, because deposits of china clay in the area were found to be the largest in the world. Demand was further increased when other uses were found for the substance. You can see the signs of this fascinating past on a visit to the China Clay Mountains of St. Austell, known as the Cornish Alps. One of Cornwall's most famous visitor attractions, the Eden Project, sits in the site of a former clay pit.

Inside The Eden Project - Andy & Sue Caffrey

Cornish Diaspora

Diaspora: The place where these people live. The movement, migration, or scattering of a people away from an established or ancestral homeland.

A Strong Sense of Identity

The people of Cornwall have always had a strong sense of identity. They have long fought to be recognised as an ethnic group in their own right. In 2014 they achieved that goal, when the Cornish were granted minority status under the European Framework Convention for the Protection of National Minorities, giving them recognition as a distinct ethnic identity. This means that the Cornish will be afforded all the same protections as the Welsh, Scottish and Irish. Government departments and public bodies must take Cornwall's views into account when making decisions. The change also helps to protect Cornwall's culture and identity.

The Duchy of Cornwall

Did you know that Cornwall is a royal duchy? It is one of only two royal duchies in England. Its current duke is the Prince of Wales.

Tourism Then & Now

While Cornwall was once known for its industrial prowess rather than its cream teas, it is now recognised as one of the most popular destination for tourists. Cornwall welcomes around five million visitors a year.

In fact, the numbers hit an all-time high in 2014. The railways played a big part in enabling people to get to Cornwall in the 19th and 20th centuries. Newquay was one of the first towns which adapted to the needs of visitors and is still hugely popular

Newquay Harbour - iStock

The Unofficial Cornish National Anthem

Being part of the UK, Cornwall can't have its own official national anthem. However, it does have a couple of contenders for the title of unofficial national anthem. The most popular choice seems to be *'Trelawny'*.

Based on *'The Song of the Western Men'* by Robert Stephen Hawker, a clergyman of the 1800s, it tells the story of a bishop held prisoner in the Tower of London by King James II. Trelawny was born in Pelynt. His father, the 2nd Baronet of Trelawny, supported the Royalist cause during the Civil War.

Trelawny - excerpt

A good sword and a trusty hand!
A merry heart and true!
King James's men shall understand
What Cornish lads can do!

And have they fixed the where and when?
And shall Trelawny die?
Here's twenty thousand Cornish men
Will know the reason why!

Chorus:
And shall Trelawny live?
And shall Trelawny die?
Here's twenty thousand Cornish men
Will know the reason why!

Another song which some argue is the 'Cornish national anthem' is *'Bro goth agan tasow'* ('Old Land of our Fathers'). This uses the same tune as the anthem of Brittany, *'Bro Gozh ma Zadoù'*, and the Welsh national anthem, *'Hen Wlad Fy Nhadau'*.

Humour

Q: What's a Cornishman's idea of a balanced diet?

A: A pint of scrumpy in each hand.

A gang of robbers broke into the Truro Lawyers' Club by mistake. The old legal lions put up a fierce fight for their lives and their money. The gang was happy to escape in one piece.

'It ain't so bad,' one crook said. 'At least we got fifty quid between us.'

His boss screamed at him, 'I warned you to stay clear of lawyers… we had £200 when we broke in!'

Many years ago, a tin miner fell down a shaft in the Geevor mine.

The deputy shouted, 'Ess anythin' brokun?'

'Naw,' he replied, 'there's nawthen down 'ere but a few rocks.'

Q: What do surfers do when they see each other?

A: Wave.

A tourist from West Virginia is on the Torpoint Ferry crossing into Cornwall for the first time. Upon seeing some seagulls, he says to the man next to him, 'Them's darned pretty birds.'

The Cornishman says, 'Them's gulls.'

'Well,' says the American, 'gulls or boys, them's darned pretty birds.'

A man walks into the fishmongers in Port Isaac carrying a halibut under his arm. 'Do you make fishcakes?' he asks.

'Of course,' says the fishmonger.

'Oh good,' says the man. 'It's his birthday.'

Q: What was Camelot famous for?

A: Its knight life.

A tourist, loaded with expensive fishing rods and equipment, approaches an old fisherman sitting on the bank of the River Lynher.

'I say, old man,' says the emmet, *'is this river any good for fish?'*

'It must be,' said the Cornishman. *'I can't get any of them to leave it.'*

A police officer sees a man driving around Launceston with a pickup truck full of otters. He pulls the man over and says, *'You can't drive around with otters in this town! There's a wildlife centre in North Petherwin; take them there immediately.'*

The man says, *'OK, officer'* and drives away.

The next week, the officer sees the man still driving around with the truck full of otters, and they're all wearing sunglasses. He pulls the man over and says crossly, *'I thought I told you to take those otters to the Tamar Otter and Wildlife Centre last week.'*

The man replies, *'I did and they loved it, so today I'm taking them to the beach at Carbis Bay.'*

It was a quiet night in Hayle and a man and his wife were fast asleep, when there was an unexpected knock on the door. The man looked at his alarm clock. It was half past three in the morning. *'I'm not getting out of bed at this time,'* he thought and rolled over.

There was another louder knock.

'Aren't you going to answer that?' asked his wife irritably.

So the man dragged himself out of bed and went downstairs. He opened the door to find a strange man standing outside. It didn't take the homeowner long to realise the man was totally drunk.

'All right, me 'nsome?' slurred the stranger. *'Can you give me a push?'*

'No, I'm sorry, I most certainly can't. It's half past three in the morning and I was in bed,' said the man and he slammed the front door.

He went back up to bed and told his wife what happened.

'That wasn't very nice of you,' she said. *'Remember that night we broke down in the pouring rain on the way to pick the kids up from the babysitter, and you had to knock on that man's door to get us started again? What would have happened if he'd told us to get lost?'*

'But the man who just knocked on our door was as drunk as a perraner,' replied her husband.

'Well, we can at least help move his car somewhere safe and sort him out a taxi,' said his wife. *'He needs our help.'*

So the husband got out of bed again, got dressed and went downstairs. He opened the door but couldn't see the stranger anywhere, so he shouted, *'Hey, do you still want a push?'*

In answer, he heard a voice call out, *'Yes please!'*

So, still unable to see the stranger, he shouted, *'Where are you?'*

'I'm over here, me 'ansome,' the stranger replied, *'on your swing.'*

A bookdealer in Lostwithiel has discovered the manuscripts for some unpublished, unexpectedly modern sequels by famous Cornish writers, including Daphne Du Maurier's My Cousin Rachel's Second Home and William Golding's Lord of the Flies from Newquay.

An elderly couple from Camborne are sitting at the dining table in their semi-detached house talking about making preparations for writing their wills. Bill says to his missus, *Edna, 'I've been thinking, my dear, if I go first to meet me maker I don't want you to be on your own for too long. In fact, I think you could do worse than marry Colin in the chemist's or Dave with the fruit stall in the market. They'd provide for you and look after you when I'm gone.'*

'That's very kind of you to think about me like that, Bill,' replied Edna. *'But I've already made my own arrangements!'*

Two Cornish farmers, who offer farmhouse bed-and-breakfast stays, are enjoying a pint in their local in Zennor. One says to the other, *'I'll tell 'e, I'll be glad when they furriners stop cummin' fer the summer.'*

'Ayse,' agrees the other. *'Then I can shave meself, taake me trouser bottoms out o' me boots and stop chewing straw.'*

Have you heard about the latest machine in the arcade in Truro city centre?

You put fifty pence in and ask it any question and it gives you a true answer.

One visitor from Devon tried it last week.

He asked the machine, *'Where is my father?'*

The machine replied: *'Your father is fishing on the River Tamar.'*

'Well,' he thought. *'That's daft for a start because my father is dead.'*

So he tried again. *'Where is my mother's husband?'*

The reply came back, *'Your mother's husband is buried in Tiverton, but your father is still fishing on the Tamar.'*

A Cornishman is driving through Devon, when he passes a farmer standing in the middle of a huge field. He pulls the car over and watches the farmer standing stock-still, doing absolutely nothing. Intrigued, the man walks over to the farmer and asks him, *'Excuse me, sir, but what are you doing?'*

The farmer replies, *'I'm trying to win a Nobel Prize.'*

'How?' asks the puzzled Cornishman.

'Well,' says the Devonian, *'I heard they give the prize to people who are outstanding in their field.'*

Ghost Stories

TALES OF THE SUPERNATURAL TO CHILL THE BLOOD

Many of us were introduced to ghosts by CHARLES DICKENS in A Christmas Carol with the Ghost of Christmas Past, followed by the Ghost of Christmas Present and finally the Ghost of Christmas Yet to Come.

A Christmas Carol was published on 19 December 1843. Early that year Charles Dickens had visited Cornish tin mines where he saw children working in appalling conditions, an experience that was later reflected in his writing, and one wonders whether he also heard tales of the ghosts that inhabit Cornish tin mines… The ghosts were known as **Knockers**, and were said at the time to be the spirits of Jews who had crucified Christ and were forced to work in Cornish tin mines as punishment.

The Duchy of Cornwall is internationally known for its ghosts, and many consider it to be the most haunted place in Britain. Myth, legend and folklore create the perfect backdrop for the creepy happenings in Celtic Kernow. Eerie sounds of bells and the heavy tread of the boots of deceased miners are heard, and all manner of manifestations, from headless horses to a white rabbit, have been seen. While some sightings turn out to be somewhat less spooky than was first thought when the truth is revealed, it is worth repeating what the novelist ANNA ELIZABETH BRAY (1826–74) was quoted as saying: *'A real old Cornish house without a ghost is an impossibility, and the true believer in the mystic will scorn the prosaic idea of rats as a solution to mysterious sound…'*

In October 1885 the Royal Cornwall Gazette printed the following advice on the subject of ghost-seeing given by a hardened sceptic to a young friend: *'My dear boy, if a ghost comes in at the door, take a pistol; if he comes up from the floor, take a pill.'*

GHOSTS ALONG CORNISH COASTS

There are more than 400 miles (700 km) of remarkable Cornish coastline with dramatic cliffs, secret coves, spectacular beaches, breathtaking bays and amazing surf. The coastal scenery is varied and beautiful. As well as everything nature offers there are picturesque fishing villages, engine houses, castles, inns, hotels and lighthouses.

The sea and the River Tamar make Cornwall virtually an island and give it an authentic feeling of being Celtic, which helps to maintain its unique atmosphere of myth and magic. Of course Cornwall is haunted, and yes, it is full of ghosts! To believe or not to believe is the question; some answers may lie in this journey to discover ghost stories old and new.

Before eerie stories from different

Cornish coastal locations are related, it is worth mentioning a type of haunting that happens around the shores where there have been shipwrecks and fatalities. The souls of drowned sailors appear to haunt these places and the calling of the dead is often heard. Many a fisherman has declared he has heard the voices of dead sailors hailing their own names.

Marazion

The town of **Marazion**, situated on the shores of Mount's Bay in West Cornwall, is widely famed as the gateway to St. Michael's Mount. The story of the ghost of an unknown lady who frequents the area of the town known as **Marazion Green** is well attested; she is known to hitch a ride on a horse and gallop as far as the nearby Red River before disappearing. This same lady has often been described as ghostly white when she has materialised to accompany late-night walkers before fading away into the darkness.

Looe

The Harbour at Looe - iStock

This small coastal town in the south-east of Cornwall is a busy port and a favourite location for holidaymakers who enjoy its sandy beaches. The town is divided in two by the River Looe, creating an East Looe and a West Looe.

Hopefully not many visiting tourists have seen the ill omen of a white hare in the town, running down the hill at Talland and vanishing when it reaches the *Jolly Sailor*, a West Looe inn known locally as *'the Jolly'* which is one of the oldest pubs in the country. The white hare haunting is said to be related to a young lady who committed suicide. Another apparition seen in this location is a coachman with a ponytail who wears a ruffled shirt. Finally, on a slightly different tack, it is also worth looking out to sea at Looe, because in 1949 a pair of green sea monsters resembling Chinese dragons were observed chasing fish.

POLPERRO

Polperro is a village and fishing harbour on the south-east coast, once a thriving centre for smuggling. Today it is a tourist delight with its jumble of charming cottages.

In the maze of caves at Polperro is a chamber known as *Willy Willcock's hole*. This is where a fisherman of the same name got lost in the tunnels and died of starvation. His spirit is still trying to find its way out. Many claim to have seen the ghost of the lost fisherman; others who have heard the terrible screams of Willy Willcock have said the sound is terrifying.

The *Crumplehorn Inn* is supposed to be haunted by a gentler couple, thought to be a young soldier and the girl who was his lover

NEWQUAY

Who doesn't know this tourist spot?

It is constantly in the news, and is a favourite spot for surfers. However, I wonder how many visitors are aware of the hauntings that have frequented the town over the years.

At *Trethellan Hill*, ghostly sightings had been reported for many years.

Trethellan Hill - Google Street View

During an excavation for the laying of pipes to the Pentire estate in 1900, the workmen unearthed some skeletons; those that believed in the ghosts found in the discovery a confirmation of their belief.

In the area around **Barrowfields** a headless horseman has been noted. Horse and rider appear to travel above the ground. Look out for them when walking home from the nightclub. **Trerice Manor,** on the outskirts of Newquay at **Kestle Mill**, is an Elizabethan manor house with a delightful garden. A guide book from the very early 20th century describes Trerice as an ancient baronial mansion, which the country people still declare to be haunted by the spirit of a certain passionate LORD OF ARUNDELL, known in the neighbouring village as the *'wicked lord'*. Fleeting glimpses of a phantom lady and the occasional whiff of perfume all add to the ambiance of the Manor House.

CALSTOCK

Calstock is a large village in southeast Cornwall on the banks of the River Tamar which divides Cornwall and Devon. The impressive viaduct that carries the railway branch line from Plymouth to Gunnislake dominates the village. A short way downriver is the Tudor manor house of **Cotehele**, now in the care of the National

Trust. Cotehele, like many of the excellent manor houses in Cornwall, has its own reports of hauntings. An ethereal young lady dressed entirely in white is said to linger here, and phantom music has been reported in the oldest part of the manor house. Mining was an important industry in the Calstock area, especially in the late 19th century after the discovery of copper in the local vicinity. Like many dangerous bygone industries, something lingers from it in the present. On one of the roads leading into Calstock a pare (group) of miners carrying candles and dressed in old-fashioned traditional work clothes has been sighted, according to local reports.

WADEBRIDGE

Wadebridge is a north Cornwall town that bestrides the River Camel, with a bridge that was built over the original wading crossing in the 15th century. The bridge has seventeen arches along its 320-foot length and is well worth a visit.

Wadebridge has numerous eerie stories. One that has been told many times and is certainly worth mentioning again is an anniversary haunting. On 31st December, at midnight, a phantom coach materialises in the courtyard of the 16th-century coaching inn, the *Molesworth Arms Hotel*. The creepy coach leaves via the hallway; it is drawn by four horses and driven by a headless coachman. Several people claim to have seen it while others say they just heard it. It could be worth checking out on a New Year's Eve at the midnight hour!

Phantom coaches are definitely popular in and around this old market town. On the night of a full moon another apparition of a coach and horses is reputed to race across Trewornan Bridge.

Egloshayle Church, situated on a

Molesworth Arms Hotel - Ian-S

road beside the **River Camel**, faces across to the town of Wadebridge. Despite the church having a strong bellringing tradition, this does not seem to have frightened away the ghostly white rabbit that some claim to have seen gambolling around the churchyard before disappearing into the wall.

As traditions go, where there are rabbits there will be someone who wants to take a potshot at them. A local man with a shotgun went out hunting the ghostly rabbit at Egloshayle Church. A few of his friends who were curious about how he would get on followed at a safe distance. They heard the gun go off and raced to the scene, only to find the hunter dead, shot by his own gun. The ghost of this tragic victim now haunts the churchyard. It can be seen pointing a gun at something disturbing the long grass in the distance.

Cornish LEGENDS

The Piskies

Piskies are little people; the Pisky has been described as a fairy, a pixie or an elf, so if you imagine something somewhere between the three you won't be far off.

The **Pisky** is mischievous and at times can be very antisocial. However, the things it does against mankind are usually done for its own fun. A favourite trick of the pisky is to entice people into bogs. It does this at night by appearing in the form of a cottage window light or a man carrying a lantern. Piskies always seem to find a way to get a person lost – hence the expression of being *'pisky-led'*.

Piskies also like to plague farmers by riding their horses into the ground, or by chasing cows so that their milk dries up. One way to detect if a tired horse had been ridden hard by the piskies during the night is to examine its mane. If the mane has been knotted into pisky stirrups, this is a sure sign. By counting the number of stirrups in the mane one could determine how many piskies had ridden the horse at any one time. Up to twenty piskies riding one horse is quite common.

Those who have had personal experience with the piskies say they are a very merry lot, always laughing, which accounts for the phrase *'to laugh like a pisky'*.

If any of the above is a worry to would-be travellers to Cornwall, there is one way to protect oneself from being pisky-led: wear your coat inside out. If you see someone wearing their coat inside out it does not mean that they dressed in a hurry; it's just that they are protecting themselves against the piskies!

The Standing Stones of Cornwall

The landscape of Cornwall is marked by many fascinating standing stones. As ancient as they are beautiful, many of these landmarks are sources of enduring local legends.

The Hurlers of St. Cleer

The wonderfully named **Hurlers** are a group of stones on Bodmin Moor dating from about 1500 BC. It is said that these curious forms are the remains of a group of men turned to stone after refusing **St. Cleer's** orders for them to stop playing hurling on a Sunday and to go to church!

Men Scryfa

'Men Scryfa' means *'inscribed stone'*. This evocative standing stone is located along a footpath called the *Tinner's Way*. The inscription it bears is in Latin, *'Rialobrani Cunovali Filii'*, which translates as *'Rialobran, son of Cunoval'*. Many believe that it is the tombstone of a king killed in the Battle of Gendhal Moor in the 6th century. The stone stands at an impressive nine feet high. The story goes that the king was the same height as this. The legend also states the king is buried beneath the stone, along with his weapons and worldly valuables.

Mên-an-Tol

Close to **Madron**, on the Land's End peninsula, you will find three upright stones made of granite. One is round with a hollow circle with the other two (of a more traditional

The Hurlers – iStock

Men-An-Tol – iStock

standing stone shape) standing on each side of it. While it is known by the dramatic name of the **Devil's Eye**, it is now thought to have been a very early kind of astronomical viewing point. Locally, the **Mên-an-Tol** is known as the *Crick Stone* because it is thought to have helped heal people who have a crick in their back, thanks to its piskie guardian!

Because of the round shape of the stone with the hole, it had a reputation for being able to help fertility. The story went that if a woman passed through the hole seven times backwards at full moon, she would soon become pregnant.

The other legend about the stone was that passing through it would cure rickets. This meant that for many years children were passed through the hole nine times for protection against the condition.

The Merry Maidens and the Pipers

Close to Land's End at Boleigh stands an impressive group of nineteen stones in a large circle, the **Merry Maidens**. Close by stand the **Pipers**, two huge granite standing stones. The legend goes that the stones are really nineteen girls who had been on their way to church when they were distracted by two pipers playing a dance! They were drawn into dancing but suddenly a thunderbolt appeared as a punishment for them dancing and piping on a Sunday! This is why the maidens and the pipers now stand still for ever!

The Pipers are the largest menhirs still standing in Cornwall, measuring an impressive 13 and 15 feet in height; around four metres.

King Arthur and Cornwall

The legendary **King Arthur** is closely associated with Cornwall. In the 12th century, **Tintagel** was described by GEOFFREY OF MONMOUTH as the place of Arthur's conception in his book, the *Historia Regum Britanniae*. While the picturesque castle ruins at Tintagel date from the 11th century, there are signs of a far earlier settlement. Below the castle ruins there is an atmospheric cave, known as *Merlin's Cave* because it is believed to be where the wizard lived. In fact, the magician is said to haunt it to this day! At the time of writing, Cornwall Council have approved plans by English Heritage to build a £4m bridge to link the mainland and Tintagel Castle. As you would expect for a change to such an ancient and well-loved site, the plan is not without controversy.

Peninsula of Tintagel Island and legendary castle ruins - iStock

King Arthur sculpture by Caroline Skelton - Rubin Eynon - CC

There are several other sites in Cornwall which are said to have connections with King Arthur.

DOZMARY POOL

Dozmary Pool, a small lake on Bodmin Moor, is the location of two Arthurian legends, concerning the **Lady of the Lake** and the sword **Excalibur**. Locals say that it is where **Sir Bedivere** threw Excalibur after Arthur's death. In 2017, a schoolgirl was paddling in the lake

Dozmary Pool - iStock

with her father when she discovered an old sword with a four-foot blade! However, on closer inspection, the sword was identified as being only around twenty to thirty years old and so is much more likely to be a lost film prop than the sword of King Arthur!

Castle Killibury

Legend tells how the Iron Age hill fort, **Kelly Rounds** or **Castle Killibury**, is actually *Kelliwic*, which played a crucial role in the Battle of Camlann, King Arthur's final battle.

The Loe

At 50 hectares or 120 acres, **The Loe**, also known as **Loe Pool**, is Cornwall's largest natural freshwater lake. This is another place into which it has been suggested that Sir Bedivere threw *Excalibur*. Tennyson wrote about Loe Pool being the location of this event in his poem cycle, *Idylls of the King*.

Cornish Recipes

The recipes of Cornwall are a part of its culinary heritage. The food experienced in the Duchy is one of the most talked-about subjects for locals and for those visiting on holiday. The cuisine that is a way of life here also reflects the rich tapestry of Cornish history. As Cornwall is surrounded on three sides by sea, the fishing industry has always been one of the main elements of the economy.

Fish and crustaceans such as crab and lobster are still a vital part of Cornish life today and a variety of seafood is as popular as ever. Mining in Cornwall helped to develop the ultimate all-in-one meal, the iconic Cornish pasty. The crimped edge of the pasty could be held by miners with dirty hands and be given to the *Knockers* (the mine spirits) if considered unfit to eat. Many varieties of filling now exist for the pasty.

The Cornish Pasty - iStock

THE CORNISH PASTY DOESN'T NEED ANY INTRODUCTION. HOWEVER, TO GET THE BEST RESULTS, ALWAYS AUSE LOCAL ORGANIC VEGETABLES AND BUY YOUR MEAT FROM A LOCAL BUTCHER. ASK FOR SKIRT, CHUCK OR PASTY MEAT.

Cornish Pasty

MAKES 2 PASTIES

Ingredients:

For the pastry:

1 lbs / 450 grams flour

5 oz / 125 grams of lard

Pinch of salt

Drop of water to mix

For the filling:

1 lbs / 450 grams of the meat of your choice

1 lbs / 450 grams potatoes

1 lbs / 450 grams swede

1 small onion

1 oz / 25 grams butter

Bit of fresh parsley

Salt and pepper

Preparation:

1. Make the pastry, cut into two pieces and roll out around a ¼ inch /6 cm thick.
2. Put a ten-inch dinner plate on top of each piece of pastry and cut around it.
3. Prepare the potatoes and swede by cutting into small pieces.
4. Chop up the onion.
5. Cut the meat into small cubes, and discard any fat.
6. To make it easier, put the rolling pin under one half of the rolled-out pastry rounds.
7. Layer the vegetables onto the lower half of the pasty round.
8. Add salt and pepper to taste.
9. Add the meat with knobs of butter.
10. Dampen the edges of the pastry.
11. Fold the top half of the pastry over into a semicircle pasty shape, pinch together and crimp to give the pasty that genuine Cornish look.

12. Repeat with other pasty round.
13. Put both pasties onto a floured tray.
14. Make a ventilating slit in the lid of the pasties.
15. Bake in a preheated oven for 1 hour at 200°C/400°F/gas mark 6.

Many different fillings can be used for the pasty, but the customary pastry is the same. Keep Cornish traditions going: identify the pasty to its owner, by marking the initial of whom each pasty is for in one corner; by doing this if there is any variation for personal taste the pasty can be recognised. Eat the pasty the Cornish way: hold it in the hand, and begin to eat it from the opposite end to the initial, as should you then leave a corner of pasty for supper it can still be identified as yours.

Dippy

A TRADITIONAL CORNISH DISH THAT IS NOT VERY LIKELY TO BE FOUND IN THE UPMARKET FISH RESTAURANTS THAT ARE A FEATURE OF MODERN CORNWALL. DIPPY IS A GREAT SUPPER DISH, EASILY PREPARED AND COOKED IN ONE POT.

INGREDIENTS:

6 pilchards
6 medium-sized potatoes
300ml of single cream
Salt and pepper to season to taste

1. Gut, scale and clean the pilchards; pat dry to finish.
2. Peel and cut up the potatoes into small cubes.
3. Put both in a saucepan and season to taste with salt and pepper.

4. Pour the cream over the fish and potatoes.
5. Simmer for around 20 minutes until the potatoes are soft and the fish is cooked through.
6. Serve with a cooked green vegetable as a side dish to complete this tasty treat.

Saffron Cake

Saffron is a spice derived from the flower of Crocus sativus, commonly known as the saffron crocus. It is believed that the Phoenicians brought saffron over with them when they came to trade for tin in Cornwall. *'As dear as saffron'* is a phrase that is often used in the Duchy; obtaining 1 lb (450 grams) of dry saffron requires the harvesting of some 50,000 flowers. When the author of this recipe left school in 1959 and went to work in a grocery shop, a dram of saffron cost one shilling and sixpence (7.5 new pence) and a one-pound tin of saffron was the most expensive item in the shop, at almost £20. Sliced saffron cake, sometimes spread with butter, and saffron buns are still very popular in Cornish households. Large saffron buns, about the size of a tea plate and known as tea treat buns, are associated with Methodist Sunday School outings or activities.

INGREDIENTS:

½ dram / 1 gram saffron
2 lbs / 900 grams flour
1 lb / 450 grams butter
4 oz / 100 grams sugar
1 lb / 450 grams currants
1 oz / 25 grams yeast
2 ozs / 50 grams finely chopped candied peel
1 pinch salt
1 tablespoon warm milk

1. Cut up the saffron strands, soak in a small amount of hot water, cover and leave to infuse overnight.
2. Rub the butter in the flour; add the salt, sugar, peel and currants.
3. Warm a little milk; pour it over the yeast and one teaspoonful of sugar in a basin.
4. When the yeast rises, pour it into a well in the centre of the flour. Cover it with a light sprinkling of the flour. After about 10 minutes the yeast rises through this.
5. Then mix by hand into a dough adding milk as needed, as well as the saffron water.
6. Leave in a warm place and let it rise for a while.
7. Bake in a cake tin for about 1 hour at 180°C/350°F/gas mark 4.
8. Turn out onto a wire rack to cool.

Cornish Splits

THESE NEVER FAIL TO PLEASE. THEY CAN BE CUT OPEN WHEN HOT AND SPREAD LIBERALLY WITH BUTTER, OR WHEN COLD CAN BE SERVED WITH JAM AND CORNISH CLOTTED CREAM. ANOTHER OLD FAVOURITE WAS TO CUT THEM OPEN, SPREAD THEM WITH CORNISH CLOTTED CREAM AND THEN SPRINKLE WITH GRANULATED SUGAR.

Cornish Split

INGREDIENTS:

1 lb / 450grams flour
½ oz / 12 grams yeast
1 oz / 25 grams butter
½ oz / 12 grams caster sugar
1 pinch salt
½ pint / 285 ml of milk

1. Warm the milk.
2. Cream the yeast and sugar together and add the milk.
3. Sieve the flour and salt together.
4. Melt the butter and add it along with the yeast, sugar and milk mix.
5. Knead and leave the dough to rise for about 45 minutes in a warm place.
6. Knead again and shape the dough into round balls on a greased baking tray.
7. Bake for about 15 minutes at 200°C/400°F/gas mark 6.

Cornish Language

The Cornish language has a fascinating history. Cornish is one of six Celtic languages, brought over when the Celts migrated across to Britain and Ireland from mainland Europe. Cornish was spoken in Cornwall, the Isles of Scilly and, to a lesser extent, in West Devon and Exeter. The Reformation of the English Church had a significant impact on the future of the Cornish language. Edward VI sent commissioners to force local people to use the Book of Common Prayer, but they were met with riots. The Cornish sent a letter to the King, declaring that *'We, the Cornyshe men, whereof certain of us understande no Englyshe, utterly refuse thys newe Service.'* With the king giving no clear response, 6,000 people marched on Exeter, leading to battles in which about 5,000 Cornish died. It is believed that before these events, Cornwall had been largely Cornish-speaking as far as Bodmin.

Sadly, by the 19th century, Cornish had died out as a spoken community language. Thankfully, from the 1900s onwards, interest in preserving and unifying the Cornish language began to gain momentum. It was recognised that it would be beneficial to agree a standard version of the language for public life and to be taught in schools. This led to the adoption of a standard written form. Since then, the number of people learning and using the language has escalated, with Cornish receiving official recognition as a minority language in 2002 under the Council of Europe's Charter for Regional or Minority Languages.

Cornish Words and Phrases

A

Abear – Endure or dislike, *'I can't abear 'im'*
Abroad – open
Abroad – to take abroad means to take apart
Actions – pretending, *'lots ov actions weth shay'*
Addled – cracked, *'tha agg es addled'*
Adventurers – those who have shares in a mine

B

Baint – is not
Baisly – dirty, unclean
Bal – a mine
Baldag – to be spattered with slime from a mine
Bee-butt – a bee hive
'Bettur a small fesh than a emptay desh' – better a small fish than an empty dish (a little is better than nothing)

C

Cabby – wet, sticky, dirty or untidy
Caddle – to do housework in an untidy manner
'Caan't call 'im 'om' – I can't remember who he is
Chacking – thirsty, very dry, in need of a drink

D

Dear es saffern – very expensive; sold by the dram, saffron was the most expensive item in a grocer's shop
Deep es Dolcoath – a secretive person; Dolcoath was the deepest mine in Cornwall

Desh ov tay – a cup of tea

Didjan fer tha knockers – a morsel of food or a corner of a pasty left to appease the spirits or little people in a mine in the hope they would lead the miners to a rich lode

E

Elvan – a local variety of blue quartz, porphyry

Emmet – an ant, or used to describe tourists from outside Cornwall

F

Faace like a rusticock – red in the face

Faathur – father

Fairmaids – cured pilchards

Faist – feast

G

Gallivanting – flirting

Gammuts – frolic, fun, play

Giss on – unbelievable

Glaws – dried cow dung used for fuel

Glumpy – sulky

N

Niceys – sweets

Night crow – someone who stops up late at night

Nimble es nine pence – a quick, nimble person

S

Skove – a rich and pure load of tin

Slab – Cornish range fire and cooking oven

Sleep – mildew

Y

Yaffer – heifer

Yafful – an armful, a bundle filling the grasp

FISHING

The fishing industry has always been a very important part of the Cornish economy. Within the world of fishing and fishermen, Cornish dialect and Cornish language words seemed to be naturally preserved. Maybe the isolation of some of the fishing communities played its part in this. There were four main types of fishing: SEINING, DRIFTING, LONG LINING and CRABBING.

Many fish have dialect names. These include: ANGLEMAINE *(monkfish)*, CAPEL-LONGER *(razor shellfish)*, CHAD *(a young bream)*, Dogga *(dogfish)*, and LONG NOSE *(sea pike)*.

Fishermen should never whistle on

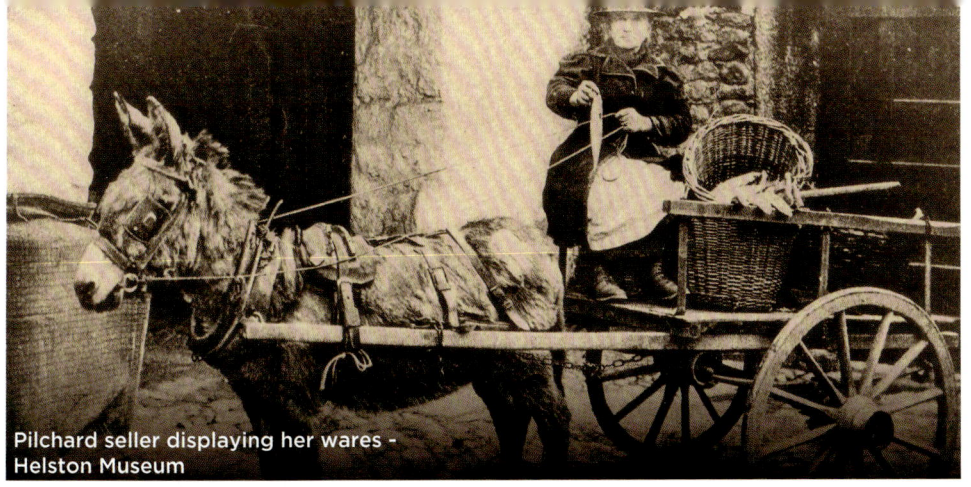

Pilchard seller displaying her wares - Helston Museum

board a boat. *Cap'n says, 'Doan't do et, cos yew'r whislun fer a gale ov wind.'*

Pilchards

Twas consider'd very unlucky ta eat a pilchard 'ead furst, es thus wud drive awaay the shoals ov pilchards ovv shore. Et es essential ta start eaten the pilcherd tail furst – thus wud then encourage the shoals ov pilchards to cum close ta shore.

Many pilchards were exported during the 18th and 19th centuries. They were salted down in the fishing areas and supplied by the thousand to Roman Catholic countries around the Mediterranean Sea, and some even went to the West Indies. This resulted in a toast from the fishermen:

Ere's 'ealth ta the Pope, may ee live ta repent

'n' add 'alf a year ta the time ov Lent,

Ta teach oall ov es cheldren fram Rome ta the Poles

Theers nuthun like pilchards fer savun theer sawls.

On economic grounds a great many pilchards went to the Royal Navy, who called them *Mevagissy ducks*.

Murder Mysteries

Famous Cornish Murders

The Murder of Nevell Norway

This true Cornish murder story involves a famous author and a strange psychic twist. It is about the murder of a man called NEVELL NORWAY which took place in 1840. Because Norway was the great grandfather of the author NEVILLE SHUTE (who wrote *A Town Like Alice*), the events of his murder continue to fascinate people to this day. It was even outlined by SIR ARTHUR CONAN DOYLE in his book, *The Edge of the Unknown*.

Norway was a high-profile and popular philanthropist and shipping merchant who lived in Wadebridge. One day as he was riding home, he was viciously attacked. His body was discovered later that day in a stream. Even though a reward of £100 was offered for information about the murder, no one came forward. A detective from London, CHARLES JACKSON, came to Cornwall to investigate. Jackson visited the place where Norway's body was found and discovered a trail of blood spots, a track which looked like it had been made by dragging a body, and footprints. Jackson spoke to a shoemaker who revealed that he had seen two men, James and William Lightfoot, hanging around an empty cottage near to where Norway was found. The next useful clue was that James Lightfoot's neighbour said that he heard him arrive home very late and say something to his wife, and then he heard them both crying. When the detective searched Lightfoot's home he discovered a pistol hidden in a hole in a ceiling beam. Both brothers were soon arrested.

The sad story then takes a weird turn. At the time of the murder, Nevell's brother, Edmund, was out at sea in his role as Chief Officer of a ship called the Orient. He had a vivid dream about the murder with all the details matching the real-life event. It seems easy to dismiss this merely as a retrospective response to a terrible event. However, not only did Edmund share the story of his dream with his fellow officers the very next day, he also made a note of it in his ship's log! Being at sea at a time well before modern communications, he didn't find out about the murder until much later on. How do you explain a man 'seeing' the events of his brother's death in a dream long before he heard about them in real life?

CHARLOTTE DYMOND

CHARLOTTE DYMONDS body was found on the banks of Rough Tor Ford.

Rough Tor Ford - CC Tim Harvey

The killing of Charlotte Dymond is another infamous Cornish murder. It attracted a great deal of attention at the time and inspired one of the age's most famous writers to capture the events in words.

Charlotte Dymond was a servant who worked at Penhale Farm, located on Bodmin Moor between Camelford and Davidstow. She was just 18 years old. The farm was owned by a widow and her son. Two other servants lived at the farm, John Stevens and Matthew Weeks, who were only a little older than Charlotte. Over time, Charlotte and Matthew formed a relationship that went beyond the professional. Charlotte was described as being pretty and confident while Matthew was said to be plain. But Matthew was not Charlotte's only admirer. Thomas Prout was the nephew of the widow who owned Penhale Farm. He sometimes worked with Matthew Weeks. The story went that another servant heard Thomas boasting that he could win Charlotte away from Matthew. Later on, it emerged that Charlotte and Thomas had been thinking about eloping.

The tragic day of Charlotte's death was a Sunday. As was appropriate for the times, everyone would have been wearing their Sunday best, including Charlotte, who had on a green striped dress and a red shawl. The very last time she was seen alive was shortly after she left the farm with Matthew Weeks, walking to the moor. That evening, Matthew returned to the farm, but he was alone. This was not unusual and all seemed OK, until time passed and still Charlotte did not return to the farm. This is when people started to wonder, especially when they noticed odd things, like the fact that Weeks's shirt was torn and his trousers were marked with mud, despite his claims that he had not gone onto the moor. Amid increasing concern, Weeks said that Charlotte had been offered a job in Blisland, a short distance away, and that she had been planning to stay at a friend's house on the way. However, when members of the household went to check the facts, they discovered that there had been no such job and Charlotte had not stayed at the friend's house. Suspiciously, Weeks left the farm that day. When his clothes were taken to be washed, some strange clues were spotted: a torn collar, missing buttons and spots of blood.

A search party discovered Charlotte's body on the bank of the River Alan. She had two cuts to her throat. A warrant was issued for Matthew's arrest. He was finally found in Plymouth at his sister's house, having planned to escape to the Channel Islands. When he was searched, the police found a pair of women's gloves and a lady's handkerchief which was marked with spots of blood. The local people were outraged by the cruel murder. Weeks was tried at Bodmin Assize Court. While he pleaded not guilty, the jury came back with a guilty verdict in just over half an hour, with a sentence of death by hanging.

However, there were some doubts. Another theory about Charlotte's death is suicide, that she killed herself to avoid what would have been the shame (in those much less enlightened times) of having a child out of wedlock. But the judge concluded that her injuries could not have been self-inflicted. There were other doubts about the eyewitnesses. Another issue was that Matthew Weeks' confession was not worded in a way that matched his personality or level of education. However, despite these doubts, Matthew Weeks was hanged for the murder of Charlotte Dymond. A monument was put up on the site where the crime was committed and reads:

This monument is erected by public subscription in memory of Charlotte Dymond who was murdered here by Matthew Weeks on Sunday April 14 1844.

The sad story of Charlotte Dymond's murder inspired Cornish author CHARLES CAUSLEY to write a poem, *'The Ballad of Charlotte Dymond'*, which begins:

> *It was a Sunday evening*
>
> *And in the April rain*
>
> *That Charlotte went from our house,*
>
> *And never came home again.*
>
> *Her shawl of diamond redcloth,*
>
> *She wore a yellow gown,*
>
> *She carried a green gauze handkerchief*
>
> *She bought in Bodmin town.*

In memory of Charlotte Dymond - CC Roger Marks

Famous *Locals*

Cornish locals have had an influence on aspects of life as diverse as music, mathematics, sport and science. With so many local people helping to shape life in the UK and further afield, we can only list a few of the notable ones here.

JOHN ARNOLD, watchmaker and pioneer of the marine chronometer

MARIA BRANWELL, mother of the Brontë sisters

W.J. BURLEY, author of the WYCLIFFE crime novels

ELIZABETH CARNE, geologist

JOSEPH HENRY COLLINS, mining engineer, mineralogist and geologist

CHARLES CAUSLEY, poet

MARK OF CORNWALL, ruler of Cornwall in the legend of Tristan and Iseult

CHARLES STANLEY CAUSLEY, CBE, FRSL was a Cornish poet, recognised for his pared-down style and associations with Cornwall. This Launceston man, while recognised in his lifetime, seems to be growing in popularity once more both in his native Cornwall and much further afield.

DAPHNE DU MAURIER, author
For many people, Daphne du Maurier is synonymous with Cornwall. Her novels, such as *My Cousin Rachel*, *Jamaica Inn* and *Frenchman's Creek*, make Cornwall a vivid and evocative setting while bringing its history to life. While du Maurier was not born in Cornwall, she and her family spent their holidays there. Not surprisingly, she settled in Cornwall and lived in

Jamaica Inn – CC Neil Howard

the county for the rest of her life. Du Maurier's books captured the magic of Cornwall so vividly that they still inspire many people to visit the area to this day.

JOHN COUCH ADAMS, co-discoverer of the planet Neptune

Mick Fleetwood - CC

MICK FLEETWOOD, musician
Born in Redruth, Mick Fleetwood is best known as the drummer and co-founder of the band *Fleetwood Mac*.

Helen Glover, Olympic gold medal winning rower

Sir William Golding, novelist

Winston Graham, novelist, author of the *Poldark* series

William Gregor, the first person to discover Titanium. The metal titanium has had a huge impact on so many industries. But it was a Cornishman who, in 1791, discovered a metal he called menaccanite.

Gregor was a clergyman and mineralogist who was born near Truro. After establishing his career as a clergyman and moving back to Cornwall with his family he began studying the chemical make-up of Cornish minerals. While another person was originally credited with the discovery of a metal he called titanium, Gregor was eventually named as the first to discover it, but the name titanium was retained.

Sir Goldsworthy Gurney, inventor. Born in 1793 near Padstow in north Cornwall, Sir Goldsworthy created his first steam-powered car prototype in the 1820s. He then went on to use the car to transport himself up Highgate Hill, London, using a lighter tubular boiler – a very important achievement. However, he exceeded that a year later when his coach travelled from London to Bath, the longest journey that any mechanised vehicle had made at the time!

But Sir Goldsworthy didn't rest on his laurels. He later went on to develop the prototype for limelight, an intense light source created by heating lime. His next achievement was to create the gas-powered Bude Light and gain the contract to light the Houses of Parliament.

John Hawkins, geologist and traveller

Barbara Hepworth, sculptor
Certain artists have come to be closely associated with Cornwall, particularly the St. Ives area. It could be argued that Yorkshire-born Barbara Hepworth

is one of the best examples of these. It was after already established artist Hepworth moved to Carbis Bay with her family that she and her artist husband Ben Nicholson became closely associated with the local art scene. Later on in her life, Hepworth bought Trewyn Studio (which is now the Barbara Hepworth Museum), to which she moved permanently following the end of her marriage. This was where Hepworth spent the rest of her life and where she made her most well-known sculptures. If you're interested in art and you get the chance to visit the museum, don't miss it. It's wonderful.

Sculpture by Barbara Hepworth

EMILY HOBHOUSE, humanitarian during the Boer War

RICHARD D. JAMES, electronica producer who works under different names, including *Aphex Twin* and *AFX*

KENNETH HAMILTON JENKIN, Cornish historian, particularly of Cornish tin mining

CHARLES ALEXANDER JOHNS, botanist, clergyman and educator

THOMAS BROWN JORDAN, engineer

DAME LAURA KNIGHT, artist and member of the Newlyn School

PETER LANYON, abstract artist

JOHN LE CARRÉ, novelist

BERNARD LEACH, potter

MICHAEL LOAM, inventor of the man engine

RICHARD LOWER, blood transfusion pioneer

This Cornishman has helped to save countless lives, thanks to his role as the inventor of blood transfusion. Born in 1631 in St. Tudy, Lower went on to become a court physician. He undertook important investigations into the circulation of the body and the nervous system and was involved in some of the earliest experiments with blood transfusions.

STANLEY LUCAS, British supercentenarian

JOHN DREW MACKENZIE, painter and illustrator, started the Newlyn Copper industry

JOHN NETTLES, actor

There's great irony in the fact that John Nettles is mostly associated with Jersey, thanks to his role in hugely popular TV series, *Bergerac*. Yet he was born in St. Austell and attended St. Austell Grammar School.

THANDIE NEWTON, actor

Thandie Newton is more closely linked with Hollywood, thanks to her hugely successful acting career, yet she grew up in Penzance.

WILLIAM NOYE, Victorian entomologist

WILLIAM OLIVER, FRS, inventor, of the Bath Oliver biscuit and a founder of the Royal Mineral Water Hospital at Bath

JOHN OPIE, portrait painter, the only Cornishman to be buried in St Paul's Cathedral

ANDREW PEARS, soap manufacturer who invented Pears soap

WILLIAM PENGELLY, geologist and archaeologist

SUSAN PENHALIGON, actress and writer

DOLLY PENTREATH, described as the last native speaker of the Cornish language

JOHN ARTHUR PHILLIPS, FRS, geologist, metallurgist, mining engineer

ROSAMUNDE PILCHER, novelist

Sir Arthur Quiller-Couch (aka 'Q'), author, academic and literary critic

Henry Chidley Reynolds, the dairy farmer who started the Anchor brand of butter

Geoffrey Rowe, Cornish comedian, better known as Jethro

Richard Sharp, rugby union player of the 1960s

Barney Solomon, rugby union player who captained the silver medal winning Great Britain team in the 1908 Olympics

Derek Tangye, author of The Minack Chronicles

Nigel Tangye, airman, author and hotelier

Richard Tangye, engineer

Roger Taylor, musician
Roger Taylor is known the world over as the drummer of the much-loved band, *Queen*. This performer, who has played to huge audiences around the world, grew up in Truro and still has a house in Helford near Falmouth.

Dame Kristin Scott Thomas, actor
Dame Kristin Scott Thomas is another Cornish local (from Redruth) who has achieved international fame thanks to her roles in films such as *Four Weddings and a Funeral, Mission: Impossible* and many others.

Richard Trevithick, inventor, engineer and builder of the first steam locomotive

Samuel Wallis, explorer

Lilian Wyles, first female detective in the British Police Force.

Local Names

Cornwall is not only the base for a number of nationally and internationally well-loved brands. It is also the source of inspiration for companies in areas as varied as fashion, food and water sports clothing! Sadly, we only have room to include some of the county's best-known brands.

Ginsters

There's no doubt that if you say the name **'Ginsters'** to most people, the first thing they will think of will be Cornwall. No wonder when Callington-based Ginsters has been selling Cornish pasties and other delicious treats since the 1960s. The company has been through a lot of changes since then. While it makes and sells a range of savouries, including sausage rolls and sandwiches, it is probably best known for its Ginsters Original Cornish Pasty which is stocked by leading supermarkets, petrol stations, convenience stores and motorway service stations across Britain. Ginsters claim that their Original Cornish Pasty is the biggest-selling product in the savoury pastry market, with no fewer than 450 million sold in twenty years!

Gul

Every water sports aficionado will have heard of **Gul**. The Bodmin-based brand has been making water sports apparel such as wetsuits since the 1960s. This is highly appropriate for a county where surfing is a big deal. Gul is credited with creating the very first one-piece wetsuit in the 1970s. This product was known in the early days as 'the steamer' thanks to the steam which exuded from it when it was taken off, because of the wearer's body heat escaping! These days, Gul makes products for other water sports such as wakeboarding, sailing and kitesurfing.

Sharp's

Rock-based **Sharp's** is one of the fastest-growing breweries in the UK. The company's best-known beer is Doom Bar, named after the famously dangerous sandbank in the Camel Estuary in North Cornwall which is known for its sometimes dramatic surf during storms. The beer won the CAMRA (Campaign for Real Ale) beer of the year award in 2004 and won a place in the world's top fifty bottled beers at the International Beer Awards in 2006.

With thanks to GUL Performance Apparel

The Natural Fibre Company

The **Natural Fibre Company** is a specialist woollen mill based in Launceston, Cornwall. It is a notable

local name for a number of reasons, not least because it is the only small-scale full-range textile mill in the UK. It is the only company in the country that spins both wool and worsted yarns under the same roof. It's also one of the few mills in the world which processes and provides yarn in small enough quantities for smaller businesses to use. The company buys raw fleece from farmers and rare sheep breeders and then processes it for sale. By doing this, it is helping to maintain awareness and use of rare-breed sheep. As well as operating the UK's only organically accredited dyeplant, The Natural Fibre Company is also part of the Campaign for Wool, which 'aims to promote wool and focuses on the sustainable attributes of wool as a natural fibre that meets an international environmental agenda'.

Seasalt

Yet another well-known name to come out of Cornwall is **Seasalt** clothing. If you're into clothes, you'll have heard of them. This thriving fashion company is based in Falmouth. Its story started when the Chadwick family went into a small shop in Penzance to buy some waterproof coats and ended up buying the shop! Later on, the company was created after the men of the family decided to start a fashion brand to celebrate what they love about Cornwall. To this day, the company includes references to the Cornish culture and landscape in its clothing range.

WEST CORNWALL PASTY COMPANY

Ginsters is not the only name closely associated with Cornish pasties. The **West Cornwall Pasty Company** is also a well-established producer and seller of the delicacy. While the company's headquarters are in Long Crendon, Buckinghamshire, its products are made in Penryn in Cornwall.

CROWDFUNDER

Newquay is more commonly associated with fun, surfing and sunshine. But these days it also has a strong connection with one of the most important phenomena to benefit new and developing businesses in the last few years – **crowdfunding**. Just in case you didn't know, crowdfunding provides a way for individuals or businesses to publicise their initiatives to the world through an online platform and gain the funding they need to bring their goals to life. One of the biggest names in that landscape is Newquay-based **Crowdfunder**, which describes itself as the UK's number one crowdfunding website. In just a short time, Crowdfunder has helped thousands of projects get off the ground as well as continuing its own impressive expansion.

Cornish Customs

As a county rich in history, Cornwall has some fascinating customs, a number of which are kept alive to this day. From the Helston Flora Day to sham mayors, dancing, singing and general merriment continue to be central to Cornwall's identity.

Helston Flora Day

Helston Flora or **'Furry' Day** takes place every year on 8th May, apart from when that date happens to fall on a Monday or Sunday. Believed to be pre-Christian, this popular spring festival aims to celebrate the end of winter and the arrival of spring. You will find many of Helston's houses and shops dressed with plants and flowers to symbolise the new life that spring brings with it. Flora Day starts early with the striking of a large bass drum at 7 a.m. The local people take part in two customs – the **Furry Dance** and the **Hal an Tow**. Around eighty couples will dance through Helston's streets, going into certain buildings to symbolise pushing out the dark of winter and inviting in the light of spring. You can only take part in the dancing by applying to the Flora Day Association and receiving an official invitation.

Flora Festival – CC Roger Allday

The **Hal an Tow** is a mummers' play which recounts the history of Helston. There are songs about the Spanish Armada, St. George and the fight between St. Michael and the devil. Those taking part wear special costumes and will also wear lily of the valley, this being one of the symbols of Helston. Back in the Victorian age, Flora Day was banned for being 'a drunken revelry'. These days it is a thriving local tradition and a popular family day out.

Allantide

Allantide (or CALAN GWAF or NOS CALAN GWAF as it is known in Cornish) is another pre-Christian Cornish festival.

This one was traditionally celebrated on the night of 31st October and the next day. Despite its early roots, it is often linked to St. Allan, a lesser known Cornish Saint. This is the reason that **Allantide** (or *Allhallowtide* as it is also known) is also known as **Allan Day**. In the past, Allantide was a popular occasion for parties across Cornwall.

The Allantide Game – CC Jane Cox

The apple was a huge part of Allantide, as you can tell from the many rituals involving the fruit. People gave large red apples known as Allan Apples to their loved ones. The day after Allan Day, young women would attempt to 'discover' the identity of their future husbands by placing an apple under their pillows and hoping for their dreams to reveal them! The apples were also given as a good-luck gift. A version of apple bobbing is also played on Allantide night. It involves candles and apples hung from nails! The Cornish Culture Association hold a campaign every year encouraging people to *'Mix a little Allantide in your Halloween'*.

Guise Dancing

Guise dancing is an old Cornish tradition which has had a resurgence in popularity in recent years. Also referred to as goosey, geese or guize dancing, this fascinating custom is practised over the Christmas period and on some other days. It is an interesting tradition which combines mumming, dancing and music. As the name suggests, guise dancing is all about disguise. From 'mock formal' style (grand old clothes from the past to parody the wealthy) to clothes covered in shreds of ribbons to dancers sporting deer horns, taking on another identity is what guise dancing is all about. Today, guise dancing features Cornish dance and a version of the old Christmas plays. Another aspect of the tradition is putting on processions. Back in the 1920s and 1930s, St Ives had a guise dance parade. Penzance has held the parades since 2007 as part of the Montol Festival. To hear a wonderful first-hand memory of guise dancing in the 1930s, visit the Cornish Memory website at **http://cornishmemory.com/item/GUN_RTR_345b.**

Mock Mayors

In many parts of Cornwall, the local people elect a 'mock' mayor at festivals and feast days. Mock or sham mayors were an early form of political satire, sending up and subverting those in power. They were popular figures in many local communities. A well-known version of this was the **Mayor of the Quay** in Penzance. Another is the **Mayor of Mylor**, a mock mayor tradition from Penryn. We have already looked at the Helston Flora Day dance and apparently a mock mayor was also elected during that event. Sadly, this was banned during the Victorian times. The best known of the sham mayors was at Penryn. He had grand regalia and 'mock officers', including two mace bearers

Mayor and Mock Mayor speeches at the modern Golowan Festival – CC Reedgunner

who carried large cabbages instead of the more traditional ornamental staffs! On occasion, the light-hearted mockery became too much for the actual mayors. One Cornish historian recorded an incident in which the real Mayor of Penryn sent police officers to confront the mock mayor. However, the sham mayor immediately ordered the real mayor and his people to be locked up overnight, which was duly done! With both Penzance and Polperro having revived their mock mayor traditions, this ancient custom can still be enjoyed today.

Cornish Sports

With such strong roots in its past, it is perhaps not surprising that Cornwall has some fascinating sporting traditions. Whether it is wrestling or windsurfing, the sports that are popular in Cornwall are closely connected with its heritage and landscape.

Cornish Wrestling

Cornish wrestling – or *'wrasslin'* or *'omdowl Kernewek'*, as it is known locally – is popular in Cornwall and has been for many centuries. It is believed to go all the way back to the 1100s when a warrior called Corineus wrestled a Cornish giant called Gogmagog, on a cliff top. It is so important to Cornwall that it has its own organisation; the Cornish Wrestling Association was formed in 1923. Its motto is: **Gwary Whek Yu Gwary Tek: Good Play Is Fair Play.** At the Battle of Agincourt in 1415, Cornwall's soldiers bore banners which held pictures of wrestlers. In 1520, when King Henry VIII met with Francis I of France near Calais, they marked their connection with events such as wrestling contests. The Cornish wrestlers were proud to win over the French. By the 19th century, Cornwall had a well-established but well-mannered wrestling rivalry with Devon. Devon men had a technique called 'out-play' in which they kicked and tripped up their opponents. Many people turned up to watch Cornwall versus Devon, with large bets being made. Thanks to Cornish tin miners emigrating for work, Cornish wresting spread to many other parts of the world in the 19th century. If you search

Cornish Wrestling - CC

for 'Cornish wrestling' on YouTube, you can find fascinating footage from the old days!

When you participate in Cornish wrestling, your goal is to throw your opponent, from a standing-up position. The sport even has its own special language. The moves have names such as the *Fore Hip, the Fore Crook, the Back Crook, the Under Heave, the Knock Back, the Flying Mare* and *the Heel*. You're not allowed to grapple with your opponent or hold them down on the ground.

Cornish wrestling has its own dress code too. Cornish wrestlers either have bare feet or wear socks, with a pair of shorts. With grasping your opponent by the jacket such a core part of Cornish wrestling, the most important part of their clothing is their canvas jacket, which is made of rough material. This is laced up at the front and has old-fashioned, baggy sleeves. Cornish wrestling matches are held usually during the summer months outside on a grassy area on a six-metre-wide ring. The 'sticklers' are the referees of the Cornish wrestling world. Usually ex-wrestlers, they carry walking sticks to help them make sure the rules are being followed. They make the absolute final decision on who has won and there is no comeback from the participants. *'Wrasslin'* has undergone a revival in Cornwall in recent years. Nowadays, you can find competitions open even to newcomers.

Cornish Wrasslin'

CORNISH HURLING

Cornish hurling is the second of the two key traditional sports of Cornwall. However, this version of hurling is very different to Irish hurling. The rather poetic long name for Cornish hurling is **'HURLING THE SILVER BALL'** from the Cornish word *hurlian*. An old saying in the Cornish language goes *Hyrlîan yw gen gwaré nyi*, which, translated into English means **'HURLING IS OUR SPORT'**.

This outdoor game is played, as the name suggests, with a small silver ball. It is what is described as a 'mob' football game, a contest played between large numbers of players and between parishes. Two versions of the game were played in Cornwall. The first was *'hurling to country'*, in which the game was played between two parishes. The winner was the team that took the silver ball out of one of the parishes or into their own. In the second version of the game,

St. Ives Feast Day Mayor Silver ball

'Hurling to goal', the aim was to reach a goal on a pitch about the same size as a modern football field. In the old days, the game was particularly popular in the parishes around Newquay and Penzance. Another interesting aspect of the tradition is that the game will be stopped mid-play to allow passers-by to touch the silver ball as it is thought to bring luck or assist fertility!

Hurling has been played at the Cornish town of St. Columb Major since records started. The game takes place on Shrove Tuesday and the second Saturday afterwards. It is played on the streets and the surrounding area and local shops put up protection for their windows and doors to protect against accidents. The game is also enjoyed in St. Ives, with a children's game held in February, and in Bodmin, where a small game is played every five years.

Cornish Rugby Union

Another sport with an important place in the hearts of the Cornish people is rugby. Rugby union is a big part of the local sense of identity. The sport is hugely popular in Cornwall. Some even believe that it was the Cornish who invented rugby, thanks to a link between rugby and the games of hurling and wrestling. No wonder the motto of the Cornish Rugby Union is **Fethy Po Fyliel An Gwarry Ha Tra Nahen**, which means *'Win or lose, the game and nothing else'*.

Watersports

With its extensive coastline, no mention of sports in Cornwall would be complete without a look at surfing and water sports. Cornwall has been much loved by surfers for many years, particularly its north coast. The county is also hugely popular for sailing and water sports events held throughout the year.

Euchre

While a card game is not strictly a sport, there is one indoor game which is worth a mention here. **Euchre** is hugely popular in Cornwall. The history of the game is a little hazy, but it is thought to have Cornish roots. The theory is that it was made popular thanks to Cornish immigrants in the USA. However, another theory runs that Cornish immigrants brought it back to Cornwall from America. Either way, it is now very much a part of traditional Cornish culture. Euchre is usually a game for four players consisting of two teams. It was the first game in the world to use the joker as a gaming card.

Biography

Camilla Zajac is an author and copywriter who wrangles with words for publishers and companies in sectors as varied as engineering, telematics and manufacturing. While not a resident of Cornwall, she has been fortunate enough to spend some very happy times there doing things like wild seal spotting and attempting to learn to surf, as well as completing a student internship at the TATE GALLERY in St. Ives.

Find out more at:
www.greenlightcopywriting.co.uk